D1294216

A Day with an Airplane Pilot

by Leonie Bennett

Consultant: Mitch Cronick

BEARPORT
PUBLISHING COMPANY, INC.
New York, New York

Credits

t=top, b=bottom, c=center, l=left, r=right, OFC=outside front cover
AirTeamImages (Tomas Coelho): 15. BAA Aviation Photo Library: 11.
Cameron Bowerman: 20–21. Corbis: 4. The Flight Collection: 9, 10, 16, 17, 21t.
Brian Futterman: 19. Daniel Hamer: 12. John Kelly: 6–7.
Gary Lewis (ATCO Aviation photography): 13.

Library of Congress Cataloging-in-Publication Data

Bennett, Leonie.
   A day with an airplane pilot / by Leonie Bennett.
      p. cm. — (I love reading)
   Includes index.
   ISBN 1-59716-147-0 (library binding) — ISBN 1-59716-173-X (pbk.)
   1. Airplanes — Piloting — Vocational guidance — Juvenile literature.
   2. Air pilots — Juvenile literature. I. Title. II. Series.

TL561.B46 2006
629.132'52023 — dc22

                    2005030628

For more information, write to Bearport Publishing Company, Inc., 101 Fifth Avenue, Suite 6R, New York, New York 10003. Printed in the United States of America.

2 3 4 5 6 7 8 9 10

The I Love Reading series was originally developed by Tick Tock Media.

CONTENTS

I am an airplane pilot 4

Look at the plane 6

Checking the plane 8

Before we take off 10

Taking off 12

Flying to America 14

Pilots at work 16

Landing 18

Welcome to New York 20

Glossary 22

Index 24

Learn More 24

I am an airplane pilot

My name is Mike.

I am an airplane **pilot**.

Today I am going to fly from London to New York.

London is in England.

New York is in America.

Look at the plane

I am going to fly a jumbo jet.

I sit in the **cockpit**.

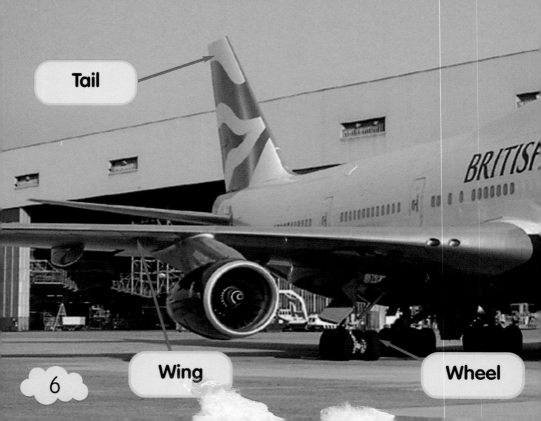

Tail

Wing

Wheel

A jumbo jet has 188 windows and 18 wheels.

Cockpit

Window

Door

Checking the plane

I need to make sure everything on the plane is working.

I check the wheels.

I check the lights.

I check under the plane.

Everything is OK.

9

Before we take off

There are two pilots.

I am the captain.

Don is the copilot.

He helps me.

Don checks the map before we take off.

I check the weather.

I also check the **controls**.

Controls

We are ready to take off.

Taking off

The plane goes down the **runway**.

Then it lifts off the ground.

The wheels go up into the plane.

Flying to America

The plane flies at 570 miles per hour (917 kph).

The **passengers** watch television.

They read books and magazines.

They eat and drink.

There are 412 passengers on this plane.

Pilots at work

I work while the plane flies.

I check the weather.

I check the fuel.

I check how fast the plane is going.

I also eat lunch in the cockpit.

It takes six hours to fly to New York.

Landing

Can I land in New York?

I must ask the people in **air traffic control**.

They check the weather.

They check the runway.

Air traffic control says I can land.

The wheels come down again.

Welcome to New York

I land the plane in New York.

The passengers get off the plane.

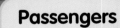

Passengers

It was a good flight.

Everyone is happy.

Glossary

air traffic control
(AIR TRAF-ik kuhn-TROHL)
people at the airport who
help the pilots

cockpit (KOK-pit)
the place at the front
of a plane where
the pilot sits

controls
(kuhn-TROHLZ)
equipment used
to fly a plane

passengers
(PASS-uhn-jurz)
the people who fly
on a plane

pilot (PYE-luht)
the person who
flies the airplane

runway (RUHN-*way*)
a special road used by
airplanes for taking off
and landing

23

Index

air traffic control 18–19

cockpit 6–7, 16

copilot 10

jumbo jets 6–7

landing the plane 18–19, 20

passengers 14–15, 20

pilots at work 4–5, 6,
8, 10–11, 16–17,
18–19, 20

runway 12, 18

speed 14

taking off 10–11, 12–13

Learn More

Jaffe, Elizabeth Dana. *Pilots.* Minneapolis, MN: Compass Point Books (2001).

Liebman, Dan. *I Want to Be a Pilot.* Ontario, Canada: Firefly Books (1999).

http://library.thinkquest.org/CR0213000/plane.htm

www.ci.phoenix.az.us/AVIATION/kids/first_flight1.html